ALL AROUND THE WORLD
AUSTRALIA

by Jessica Dean

pogo

Ideas for Parents and Teachers

Pogo Books let children practice reading informational text while introducing them to nonfiction features such as headings, labels, sidebars, maps, and diagrams, as well as a table of contents, glossary, and index.

Carefully leveled text with a strong photo match offers early fluent readers the support they need to succeed.

Before Reading

- "Walk" through the book and point out the various nonfiction features. Ask the student what purpose each feature serves.
- Look at the glossary together. Read and discuss the words.

Read the Book

- Have the child read the book independently.
- Invite him or her to list questions that arise from reading.

After Reading

- Discuss the child's questions. Talk about how he or she might find answers to those questions.
- Prompt the child to think more. Ask: The Great Barrier Reef is becoming heavily polluted. What can you do to help protect endangered areas where you live?

Pogo Books are published by Jump!
5357 Penn Avenue South
Minneapolis, MN 55419
www.jumplibrary.com

Library of Congress Cataloging-in-Publication Data

Names: Dean, Jessica, 1963- author.
Title: Australia : all around the world / by Jessica Dean.
Description: Minneapolis, MN : Jump, 2019.
Series: All around the world | Includes index.
Identifiers: LCCN 2018022797 (print)
LCCN 2018023489 (ebook)
ISBN 9781641281423 (ebook)
ISBN 9781641281409 (hardcover : alk. paper)
ISBN 9781641281416 (pbk.)
Subjects: LCSH: Australia—Juvenile literature.
Classification: LCC DU96 (ebook)
LCC DU96 .D43 2019 (print) | DDC 994—dc23
LC record available at https://lccn.loc.gov/2018022797

Editor: Kristine Spanier
Designer: Molly Ballanger

Photo Credits: Tooykrub/Shutterstock, cover; Ashwin/Shutterstock, 1; Pixfiction/Shutterstock, 3; Noradoa/Shutterstock, 4 (background); Freder/iStock, 4 (foreground); simonbradfield/iStock, 5; Oliver_Koch/iStock, 6-7tl; Matt Cornish/Shutterstock, 6-7tr; RobertDowner/iStock, 6-7bl; Maurizio De Mattei/Shutterstock, 6-7br; Daniela Dirscherl/Getty, 8-9; chameleonseye/iStock, 10; AFP Contributor/Getty, 11; kokkai/iStock, 12-13; davidf/Getty, 14-15; RainforestAustralia/iStock, 16; Thurtell/Getty, 17; James D. Morgan/Getty, 18-19; Australian Scenics/Getty, 20-21; Anya Ponti/Shutterstock, 23.

Printed in the United States of America at Corporate Graphics in North Mankato, Minnesota.

TABLE OF CONTENTS

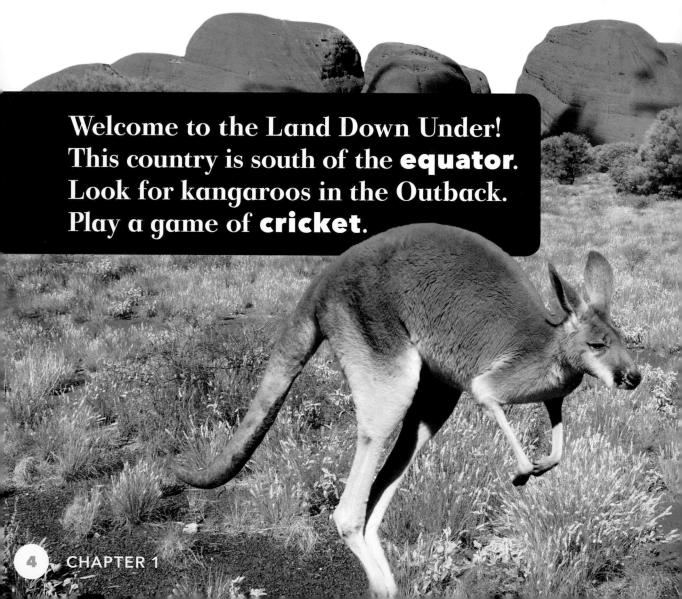

CHAPTER 1

WELCOME TO AUSTRALIA!

Welcome to the Land Down Under! This country is south of the **equator**. Look for kangaroos in the Outback. Play a game of **cricket**.

Sydney is the largest city. The Sydney Opera House is here. This is Australia!

Sydney Opera House

dingo

frilled lizard

koala

emu

Much of Australia is covered in grassland, desert, and rock formations. This is called the Outback. Dingoes race across the sand. The frilled lizard is here, too.

Areas with woodlands, shrubs, and plants are known as "the bush." Koalas live in the trees. Emus feed on seeds and plants.

DID YOU KNOW?

The lyrebird is an Australian songbird. It imitates the calls of other birds. It can also make the sounds of a cell phone. A chain saw. Even a car alarm!

The Great Barrier Reef lies along the northeast coast. It is the world's largest and longest **coral reef**. It is so large it can be seen from outer space!

The reef is home to thousands of sea animals. Like what? Tropical fish. Sea turtles. Sea snakes. Even manatees!

WHAT DO YOU THINK?

Thousands of people come every year to see the Great Barrier Reef. But it is in danger from **pollution**. Chemicals, plastics, and garbage get into the ocean. What steps could be taken to protect the reef?

CHAPTER 2
AUSTRALIA'S PEOPLE

Aboriginal people were once the only people here. They moved from place to place. They gathered food. They farmed. **Boomerangs** helped them hunt. They fished with spears.

boomerang

Torres Strait Islanders lived on nearby islands. Today, more than 600,000 people identify themselves as Aboriginal or Torres Strait Islanders. The government is working to help **preserve** their languages.

Canberra is the **capital**. The **prime minister** lives and works here. He or she is elected to run the country. Everyone 18 and older must vote. It is a law here.

Australia was a **territory** of Britain until 1901. The country still honors Queen Elizabeth II as its queen.

Canberra

TAKE A LOOK!

Each part of Australia's flag has meaning to its citizens.

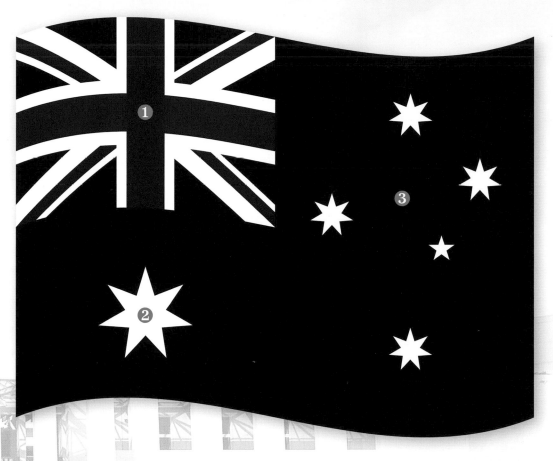

① **United Kingdom flag (Union Jack): history of British settlement**
② **Federation star: points represent states and territories**
③ **Southern Cross constellation: can only be seen from the southern hemisphere**

school
uniform

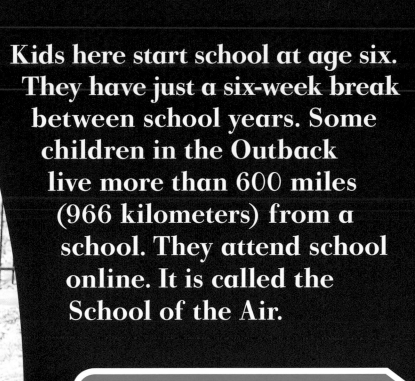

Kids here start school at age six. They have just a six-week break between school years. Some children in the Outback live more than 600 miles (966 kilometers) from a school. They attend school online. It is called the School of the Air.

WHAT DO YOU THINK?

Most children here wear uniforms to school. Do you wear a school uniform? Do you think students should have to wear them? Why or why not?

CHAPTER 3

FOOD AND FUN

Time for brekkie! This is what Australians call breakfast. Choose between cold cereal or eggs and bacon. Or try Vegemite. This is a salty spread for toast. Have a hamburger for dinner! It comes piled with tomato, bacon, pineapple, beets, egg, and lettuce.

Vegemite ····▶

Beach cookouts are common. People grill sausages. Lamb. Or crawfish.

January 26 is Australia Day. Families watch boat races and go to the beach. Fireworks light up the night sky.

Anzac Day honors soldiers of past wars on April 25. An outdoor service is followed by a parade.

Summer starts in December. This is beach time! Aussies swim and dive to see ocean life. They surf giant waves. They hike and play tennis.

Winter begins in June. Rugby and Australian-rules football are played.

Australia is a big country to explore. Would you like to visit?

QUICK FACTS & TOOLS

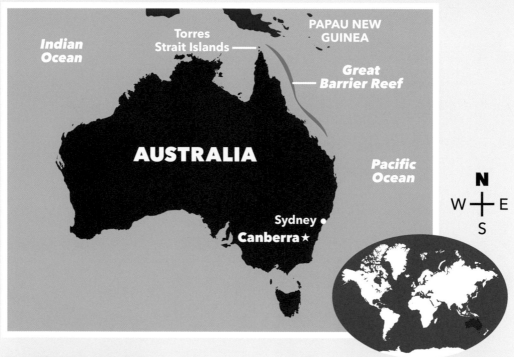

AUSTRALIA

Location: Oceania, between Indian and South Pacific Oceans

Size: 3 million square miles (7,741,220 square kilometers)

Population: 23,232,413 (July 2017 estimate)

Capital: Canberra

Type of Government: parliamentary democracy under a constitutional monarchy

Language: English

Exports: iron ore, coal, gold, natural gas, beef

Currency: Australian dollar

GLOSSARY

Aboriginal: The native people of Australia who have lived there since before the Europeans arrived.

boomerangs: Curved sticks once used as weapons and hunting tools in Australia.

capital: A city where government leaders meet.

coral reef: A strip of coral close to the surface of the ocean or another body of water.

cricket: A game played with a ball and bat.

equator: An imaginary line around the center of the Earth.

pollution: Harmful materials that damage or contaminate the air, water, and soil.

preserve: To keep alive or maintain.

prime minister: The leader of a country.

territory: The land under the control of a state, nation, or ruler.

Australia's currency

INDEX

TO LEARN MORE

Learning more is as easy as 1, 2, 3.

1) Go to www.factsurfer.com

2) Enter "Australia" into the search box.

3) Click the "Surf" button to see a list of websites.

With factsurfer, finding more information is just a click away.